Nature the Teacher

Joshua Bejoy

Published by Booksthakam in association
with Writers' Readers

Published by Booksthakam
Booksthakam India, 4B Muthoot Rainbow, AKG Nagar, Peroorkada
Thiruvananthapuram, Kerala 695005, India

info@booksthakam.com
www.booksthakam.com

NATURE THE TEACHER

A Booksthakam Book / published by arrangement with the author

ISBN-13: 9789391850005
Cover Design: Ajeesh Kumar G
Cover Image: Dr. G. Ravikanth, scientist, ATREE Bengaluru
Illustrations: Joshua Bejoy

I dedicate this book to my mother, Suma Sunny, for staying up late with me as I typed away, and giving me motivation.

Contents

Evolutionary Introduction

Sometime last year, I got an English assignment, which read:

"Do a write up on "If animals could talk".

I actually kind of liked these kinds of assignments, because I could finish one in half an hour and it seemed pretty fun writing one of them. I don't know why, but that assignment was the thing that lit a spark for this book. So, this is what I wrote:

Birds were talking amongst themselves in choked voices on how the smoke was getting on to their lungs. The ants muttered to themselves on how their anthills were swept away by last night's thunderstorm, and a crow cawing to its friends, shouting at the top of its lungs a call that it had found food. Animals now speak as we do, and now, it has raised the biggest animal rights movement ever seen. This time, though, animals are the ones who protest. A neighbour rhapsodised with you the other day about how he met a talking anaconda three years ago during his holiday, and asked him whether he could lead him to the Amazon River. It seemed that the animal was lost in a tidal bore, ended up in a ship, and it had taken him to the city suburbs of Brazil. As he had no other option, he gave the snake to an animal care centre, but now it was all history. With the animal's ability to talk, they spoke openly about the harsh conditions they were forced to live in. Tigers and Lions in captivity roared and shook the bars of the metal prison they had been kept in for so long, the monkeys go haywire, shouting partially formed sentences, the rhinos stabbing zookeepers who strayed inside their quarters and elephants trumpeting loud music through their trunks and trampling everything around them. Every day, video clips come from talking gulls and pelicans, who dived down into the water for fish, and surfaced with their talons and beaks filled with floating waste patches. They had given an appeal to clean the seas last year, but till now, the mass of garbage was ever growing. There were others too, a tiger who came out of the woods who wanted the others of his kind freed from zoos, a canary who dreamed of a world without bird sanctuaries and a rather shocking appearance was made by a dolphin who wanted to stop all traveling aquariums. Apes like orangutans learn a new way of speech, as they are humans' closest relatives, copying our manners of life in every aspect. But there have been several breakthroughs in the field of animals. Humans now understand the feelings of animals more than ever, so there is no misunderstanding between them. The work of zoo psychology has become obsolete, as now anyone can understand what an animal feels like just by asking. Now marine biologists, ornithologists and others in the field of studying animals have made a breakthrough in their careers, as they can understand speech, and can answer any questions that we have to quench our curiosity. Now animals are not captured for studying, but are asked for volunteering, or coming at their own will. Learning languages has made quite a sizeable amount of animals smarter, as they can now tell and understand in a more complex form of language, which they weren't used to before. It is a strange world, pounding with problems, and with solutions coping to be fit with everyone.

I remember myself, just sending it, being so satisfied with my project work. It was actually one of the things that inspired me to start this book.

But then, after that, I just looked closer at nature each time I saw it. I started writing down my thoughts and observations on my computer, blasting RHCP (Red hot chilli peppers) or Metallica in full volume, and reading articles about nature. After my mother read a few of my written down musings, she told me that adding a lesson with each animal, something that metaphorically matched their behaviour would be a nice idea. I was kind of reluctant at first, but then I added those too.

And here we are.

Look, this was just a book where I just wrote down my thoughts, and I'm not trying to advise anybody, since nobody likes useless advice.

And just as a little note in the end, I wanted to write a book where it would feel like the animals mentioned are talking to you while you read it. What if animals could actually talk? What if the assignment given above was true? Anyway, I just genuinely hope you enjoy the book.

1. Gargantuan Elephant

In the jungle band, the Savanna Stars,

The lion roars,

And the wild duck goes quack,

Joined with the hissing of a snake,

And the grunt of a boar.

And what does the elephant play
with the band's other four?

He plays the trumpet,

And there comes the shout "Encore".

The African elephant is the largest living land animal on the planet. They are dark grey or brown in colour and can be found in both Asia and Africa. Their eyesight is rather poor, but their large ears are sensitive to even the quietest of sounds, which enable them to sense almost everything. Elephants usually travel around in large herds, each consisting of about ten to hundred elephants. Cows (female elephants) and calves (baby elephants) are the ones who go with a herd, led by the oldest female elephant in the herd, while bulls (male elephants) leave their herd by the age of fourteen and live pretty much isolated lives. The elephant has a good memory, which helps it remember routes to shelter, water holes and places of vegetation. Elephants are usually shown in a positive light and symbolism in most cultures and they signify good luck, wisdom, strength, cordial relationships etc. Elephants are also an inevitable part of many festivals, where they are adorned with flowers, clothing, metal ornaments and paint.

Elephants are also an endangered species. As hunting and illegal poaching grew in the late 19th and the earlier part of the 20th century, the number of wild elephants decreased drastically. Hence, laws have been enacted to save the few that we now have on our planet. Elephant's teeth and tusks (also known as ivory) are valuable and are sold in black markets for staggering amounts of money. Elephants are fairly sensitive creatures, and they help and tend to each other at times. They live in a society wherein they try to understand each other the best they can, and live together in harmony. Usually, male elephants fight each other with their tusks in order to establish dominance amongst themselves.

So, what can we learn from the elephant?

The elephant teaches us to be kind and emphatic. They also teach us to care for and tend to each other, to help others out in hard times, and to move on with life, from one place to another, carrying our memories along with us.

Oh, shut up! Everybody who meets me says that!
Those must be world record size ears!
I was talking about these elephant ears
Oh yeah...........

2. The Promised Land

High in the air, where the winds don't blow fair,

I fly on hard to reach my second lair,

Over the hills and over the seas,

*I have reached it now, let's have
a night of zzzzes!*

Migratory birds are the birds which migrate long distances each year in search of more favourable climatic conditions, such as when a place is hot, they move to a cooler place, and when a place is cold, they move to a warmer place. The migration of birds such as swallows and storks have been recorded in places such as ancient Greece. The patterns of migration are not random, but they have specific time for migration and return. Unlike a fixed timetable on a pinboard, the bird's inner senses tell it to move to another place. If it has moved once, it will follow the same pattern along with its mates for the rest of its life. This repeating pattern is called a mind map. But in certain years, when the weather has a fluctuation or a sudden change, the bird's inner cycle is broken and they migrate into different places, all over the word. This sudden change is usually an explainable anomaly, such as a lack of food, changes in weather or breeding. There are several risks involved in bird migration, such as: spreading of invasive bird species across new regions, poaching of migrating birds, risk of birds getting injured or getting attacked by wild birds.

As a matter of fact, birds fly in flocks in **V** shape for a valid reason. When the birds form the V, they are in an aerodynamic shape, which is a shape that enables them to easily cut through air. When the lead bird flaps its wings, it gives off a tiny gust of air on which the second bird takes advantage of and helps it move easier. The second bird, when it flaps its wings, gives off another gust of air which the third bird uses to its advantage and so on. The tiny gust of air that the birds create is called slipstream. It helps them travel long distances without using much energy. There are many lessons that we can learn from a flock of birds, but the most significant of them is united we stand, divided we fall. The other lessons we can also pick up are to adjust to anything in any way possible, their determination to overcome adversities by investing any amount of hard work, their perseverance to keep on flying on those wings until they reach their destination and their ability to withstand anything on the way, dodging dangers. These are the abilities that help them navigate their way through the treacherous routes that are in store for them, and live to see the Promised Land.

Are you out of your @$$^^^ $#^@^&((&%$%ing mind map! Let's go to some which is more popular this season. Like how about Norway? I've heard that they have some nice chocolate over there.
You know what? Its getting kind of cold around here. Why don't we go with the sparrows to the Sahara?
COUCH POTATO
On the plus side, we can also post that on birdagram!
Yeah, but the weather over ther is as colder than it is over here!

3. Kangaroos: The king of kickboxing

As the kangaroos travel through
the desert Australian plain,

The little one thinks "There is nothing to gain,

Other than a bad knee pain!"

But the mother kangaroo does vouch,

As she sees him walk like a grouch.

"You can get onto my pouch,

And inside you can crouch,

And ride inside me like a coach!"

Kangaroos are the joey – carrying marsupials from the land down under, and wallabies are their shorter cousins. They are about six feet at their tallest, and they eat most kinds of greenery. Female kangaroos carry their young (who are called joeys) in pouches, located on their bellies. Male kangaroos kick box during the mating season, so as to show the females who the alpha males are. They use their hind legs to keep their balance, and then deliver strong blows that make the other kangaroo double over.

Kangaroo mothers are real caretakers. They clean their pouches before they welcome their joeys into the world, and when joeys do come into the world, they come as small creatures, not more than a few centimeters long. Then, they slowly develop into mature, full – size kangaroos.

So, what can we learn from kangaroos? We can learn to love and care, to protect the ones we love, and to fend for ourselves in the wild.[1]

[1] See the cartoon on the next page? Well, the kabuki mask on the left is Joey Jordinson from Slipknot.

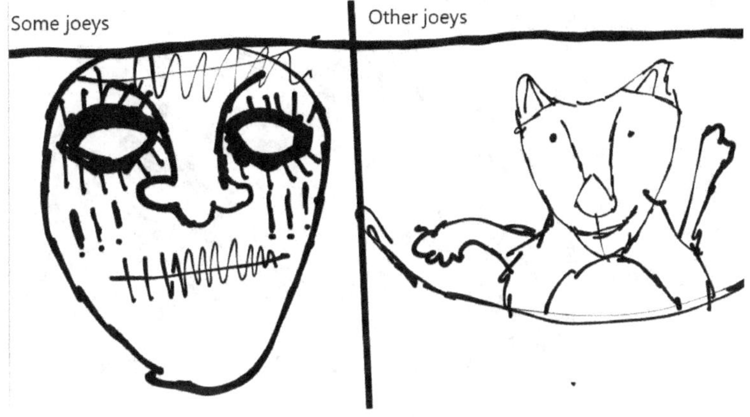
Some joeys
Other joeys

4. Immortals

As you swim through the waves, you see,

An immortal jellyfish, how good could it be?

As if you ask me how we are immortal and why,

*I don't know, but our superpowers
race sky high.*

Immortal jellyfish are one of the most fascinating creatures found on Earth. Living in the Mediterranean Sea, their life cycles are the most interesting life cycles ever. True to its name, the immortal jelly fish starts life as larva called Planulae. Planulae travel around a bit, and then settle down into the rock and grow into several polyps. From polyp, they mature and grow into jellyfishes. Hereon, the jellyfish continues its life like any other organism. The secret of its immortality lies in the fact that the jellyfish can revert to its polyp stage when threatened or when it reaches old age. This process can go on indefinitely, so biologically, the jellyfish is immortal. But usually, the jellyfishes do not reach a considerable age as they are either hunted down or die because of diseases.

So, what can we learn from the immortal jellyfish?

Immortal jellyfish are immortal, but they face as many of the same hurdles in life as we do, though they find smart ways to deal with them. But reverting to childhood, or opting rebirth.............. those are powers that we mere humans don't possess. However, we can learn to deal with our problems, barriers, and difficulties, and to move on, all from the tiny immortal jellyfish.

JOSHUA BEJOY

5. Jaws and Jugs

I look like a set of jaws, growing on a plant,

And there are no three wishes I will grant,

There is a choice of life and death,

And you must handle it all with stealth,

When you land right on my jaw,

I close my mouth, and eat you raw

Carnivorous plants might seem like an unworldly subject, limited to otherworldly fantasies, but they do exist. They either have jaws (like the Venus flytrap) or they wait for their prey to fall down into a pitfall (like the pitcher plant). This type of plant is one of the most ferocious in the world, and about 750 species are officially recognized. One of the most popular among the carnivorous plants are the pitcher plant and the Venus flytrap. The Venus flytrap is a classic open jawed monster. It usually waits for its prey to get close enough, and only then does it unleash its true colors and open its mouth and get the prey. How it senses dinner when it is near is rather a wonder. It has sensitive hairs, which tell the plant if something is in its mouth, and then it activates its reflex to close its mouth. While the prey is in its mouth, the flytrap does not open its mouth. The prey, slowly in a few hours, gets digested from the exoskeleton (depending if the prey is insect, or something else) to the flesh. It usually grows in forests, and its native habitat is in North and South Carolina. It is classified as vulnerable by the US government, due to over collection and habitat destruction. Though it is vulnerable, it is a popular house plant, and there are many greenhouses who sell them legally. Although there are many regulations concerning flytrap's sale, poachers around the world cut and take away Venus flytraps in bulk from their natural forest habitats to other places, where they sell them in black markets for high prices. The other (a little lesser known) type of carnivorous plant is the pitcher plant. At a few inches or much more, it is a wild plant like the flytrap, but unlike its fanged cousin, it can grow in sandy marshes to poor soil, whereas flytrap can't. The pitcher is shaped like a pitcher, and if you look closely, you will see that there are small spikes and a gooey wax, which holds in the insect where it has gotten stuck. The pitcher plant, in another way, is different from the flytrap, as it is more of a fall in trap than an ambush trap. It sits quietly among the grassy bushels of its surroundings, waiting for a grasshopper to jump right into their trap. After it does, the outside of the pitcher shaped plant shows no changes, but it is closed from the inside. The prey has just fallen into a burning mixture of digestive juices and water, and within a few days, almost nothing is left of the victim.

Such is the ferocity of the carnivorous plants.

Their evolution story is as interesting, as their ways of catching prey. At about the time when dinosaurs roamed every part of the planet, a genetic anomaly among a group of plants gave birth to the first generation of carnivorous plants, over centuries, they have perfected themselves in every way, in catching their prey and in alluring appearance to entice the insects with smell, rather than sight, like the sundew, which is yet another carnivorous plant, which draws the unsuspecting insects using a kind of nectar it secretes. When the insect (usually an ant, as they live underground almost everywhere) comes in contact with the plant, it gets stuck to a gooey gluelike sticky substance that keeps it in place, while the plant works its way into the insect, eating it. The strange genetic anomaly that occurred about 700 million years ago is one of the factors that has changed both human history and perception. In the earlier times, when the only literate people on the planet were monks, abnormal activity in plants and animals were indirectly connected with an evil source of power, and witchhunts ensued. The understanding of biology was not very widespread until the 1700s. In the first stages of discovering meat eating plants, people could not accept such a possibility, as science has begun to spread its influence by that time (i.e. By the mid-1800s, when things started to change for the betterment) and such things were considered only as imaginary inventions. It (the genetic anomaly) is one of the things that makes the branch of carnivorous plants a unique one. It is an extreme way of how a creature adapted to its surroundings.

The lessons that we learn from the meat eaters of the plant world are to be patient for the prey to arrive, bold to make a unique change to their own species, and being unique in our own ways.

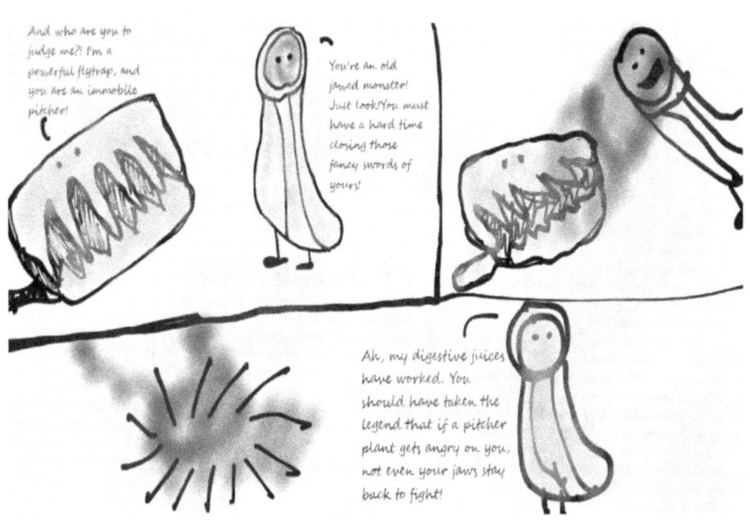

6. Fancy flower buds

After days of sun and rain,

All it came from a single grain,

*Out of the long thin shoots of the plant
blooms the bud of a flower,*

And in mid - air it does hover,

With days and nights of growing power,

Here is the result, the beautiful blooming flower

Flowers are the most attention - grabbing, yet overlooked, creations of God. Their delicate dew-covered petals, striped with lines, or single colored, lower down their bodies, their green sepals like thin armor, proud anthers atop the thin and slightly swaying filaments, and to cap them all down, a huge thick filament in the middle. The flower looks beautiful, but the struggle behind the making of such a wonderful gift of nature is curious.

It all begins with a simple seed, dug into the ground. If the requirements such as fertile soil, ample sunlight and adequate water are provided, the plant will grow fine. The process takes weeks and months. Each time the seed pushing on the darkness of the black soil above will be met with resistance from the discouraging soil trying to push it down.

But as the seed gains strength with its new addition of small roots, it peeps out and then starts growing. In about a year, the plant will be fully formed, with all of its parts functional. The plant bears leaves, long thin and green branches working its way into adulthood, fruits who bear hope that they will be the lucky ones who don't get infested by pests, and the flowers, still shy about coming out of their buds. In fact, the green coloured casing of the buds grows along with the flower and in the end becomes the flower's sepals. The flower acts as the main reproductive part of the plant, so after it is in full bloom, a few pollen grains from the anther may get dispersed by the wind onto a journey unknown.

7. Smart School of Sardines

Oh, there comes a shark, there comes a squid,

Those silly pair, how do we get rid?

*As both of them come, with their
mouths open wide,*

We split our school and take them for a ride!

*Through canyons and lagoons,
they chased us through,*

Their speed going down, their hunger grew,

And until they stopped and gave up the chase,

All because of our acrobatic tricks, want to join me for a race?

Among fish that are canned, sardines are the most popular, in consumption and in literature, it's now become more like a phrase of expressing how tightly a space is packed, referring to the way sardines were packed into small tin containers in the early 20th century, when it was fished in bulk. Though the fishes might seem pretty much dead in their tin containers, they are much more of a treat to watch in the ocean. Sardines, unlike other saltwater fish for consumption like Tuna or Salmon, are smaller in size, and they swim in huge flocks called schools. They are mainly prey to filter feeders like the whale shark and different types of whales, group hunters like sailfish, swordfish, sharks, dolphins and porpoises. Just as the pun of the smart fish living in a school goes, the sardines have a simple method of evading capture, namely, moving in large packs or schools. They travel together in tightly packed groups, and whenever any of the predators from above decide to make its move, it dives quickly into the school of fish. The school is usually formed in a circle, so the inside has space to spare. When the predator gets into the school, the sardines separate themselves into two halves like acrobats, and the predator fails to catch any food. The sardines' idea is to tire out the bigger fish who are after them. They are fast moving fish, and they have no problem twirling and swimming quickly away from their hunters.

The lesson that the sardines teach us is the importance of teamwork making the dream work, their acrobatic skills that they perform even in densely packed groups, their versatile bodies which adapt to swimming in the directions they please and the strength in their fins, which has helped their species live to this day.

8. Wavering Water- lilies

Down in the water and mud, you hid,

*From there you grew, among the green
plants, the dirt you got rid,*

You rose up from the water, looking fair,

The Sun's rays glistening the water into glare

Paintings of waterlilies have enticed our thoughts into imagining that waterlilies are the things of beauty. And true, they look beautiful in reality, dew droplets mixed with water, meditating on its thin petals, the water lily itself, floating gracefully on a calm pond. An urban recreational pond is incomplete without the image of a water lily. However, if we zoom into the scene a little bit, we can see the gnarly and muddy roots that hold the water lily together.

So, what lesson can we learn from water lilies? Well, you can never judge a book by its cover.

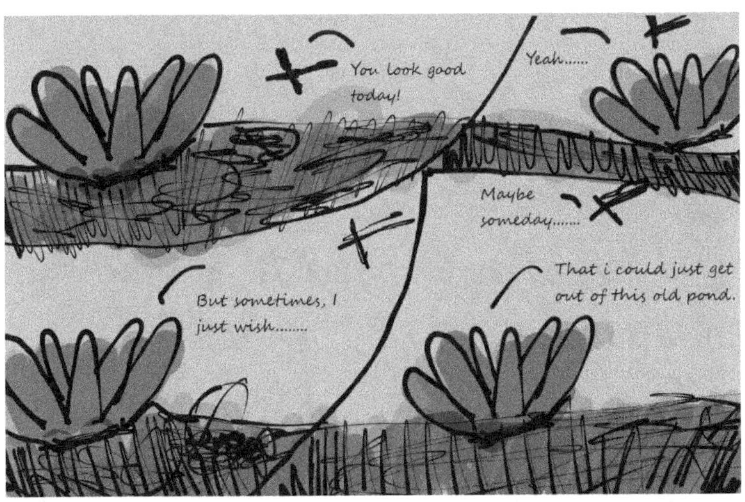

9. Animal Impartialities

Big and tough, the lion might seem,

In all his pride and glory, he will surely gleam.

Though he might seem strong and tough,

When it comes to hunting, he's just fluff

Although it might seem impossible, even animals have impartialities. Earlier in human society, men took the position of the breadwinner, while a woman stayed at home. No one did anything to change it until recently. Now, we live in an almost equal society where nearly everyone is treated equally and has the same chances as every other person. We are able to understand the differences, the things that are unfair etc as we are an advanced species who can perceive problems and work out solutions. But most animals have not reached our level of intelligence (Exceptions are monkeys, apes etc, who are only a step or two down the genetic ladder). As an example, drones (male honey bees). Their only role is to mate with an unfertilised queen bee. They don't have stingers, nor do they collect pollen. They are mostly lazy, and never go out of the beehive. As another example, male lions do not hunt as they consider it beneath their dignity. They are the ones who represent pride and they will only fight with other male lions for the other lion's land and pride, or to protect their family. As animals do not work out and change the way we do, the stereotyping has been pretty much the same from the very beginning.

So, what can we learn from lions and lionesses?

From lionesses, we can learn to do our duties responsibly, even though there is no one to cheer us on and appreciate it, and from lions, we can learn not to waste our time, and to take action, when the situation arises.

Okay, now you go up hold my honour. The human shooting crew has gone and I need dinner. They still don't know you fetch it for me! Ha HA ha!
Have you ever heard of the concepts of compassion and exercise?

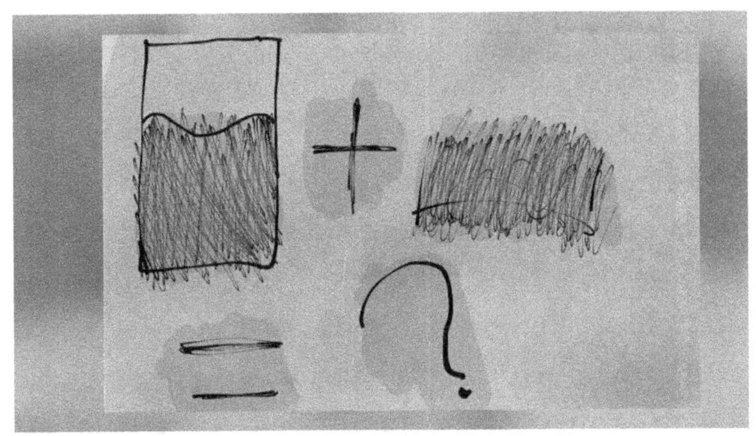

10. Merry Milkweed

I grow among other plants, cropped in a bunch,

In types I come, did you get the hunch?

Monarch butterflies come to have a feast,

And them flying around, I care the least

As you go along the road, you might see a bit of fluff flying from somewhere. It is white, and has hairs protruding from the center. The thing that you have just seen is a milkweed plant's seed. It is dispersed when the part of the plant which is responsible for making seeds breaks open or explodes. When they come out, they are clumped together in a ball, but as they fly off into the air, they disintegrate into smaller parts. There are many varieties of milkweed, such as narrowleaf milkweed, showy milkweed, whorled milkweed and purple milkweed among others. They are a rather dying species, due to human interference. When farmers try to make their soil fertile for better produce, they use an array of chemicals and fertilizers, some of which could kill the milkweed that grows amongst other cultivated plants. This is where the milkweed plant's complex system of dispersing comes to play. There are huge green pods that grow on the milkweed, and when the pod is ripe, it explodes, and expels a ball of fluff. After a few weeks, it splits into strands of thin, fluffy bits, shaped like a corona. It is very light and travels rather easily by air. This is its way of dispersing the seed over large distances. It is their way of self-preservation. Though they cannot sense approaching danger, which is a disability which has to be overlooked in this case.

The lesson we learn from the milkweed plant is to stay alive, no matter how. It is their ingenious method of survival that helped them to stay alive

on this planet.

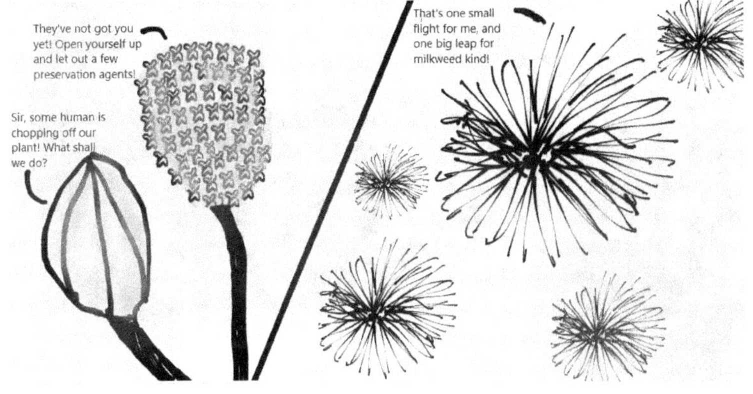

11. Bowheads and Narwhals

A tusk I have, a head, you see,

Blunt or sharp, we wade with them for free,

*But when the ice blocks our way and
life comes at a dead end,*

*We smash our way through,
for ourselves we fend*

Making way at a dead end

Among the many types of whales that roam the arctic and subarctic waters, bowhead whales are one of the types of whales who stand unique among the rest for one feature: their heads.

Bowheads are one of the largest animals on Earth, nearly next to blue whales in respect to size as they can reach up to sixty feet in length and hundred tons in weight. Their special ability lies in their huge heads. They have triangular heads, which are blunt, but are formed from the strong bone from within the skull of the whale. In fact, bowhead whales have one of the largest skulls on present day Earth. In case a bowhead whale gets stuck on thick pack ice, the bowhead gains momentum, and smashes its head against the thick ice. And as the head is presumably as hard as the ice the whale is battling with, even though without much brain, the whale can escape into the open waters with its brawn.

An equally interesting cousin of the bowhead which cannot be overlooked is the narwhal. Rather not built quite along the lines of its bigger cousin, narwhal is a medium-sized whale which is related to the beluga whale, and can grow up to thirteen to eighteen feet. Often called the unicorns of the sea, narwhals have a long spiral horn sticking out of their heads, which is actually a rather large and pointed tooth which the narwhal uses as a sensory organ and can grow up to ten feet. This "tooth" feature is more common in males than in females. They usually feed on krill and fish that come aplenty in the cold waters of Canada, Greenland, Norway and Russia.

The huge protruding tusk that rises from the whale's forehead is mainly used in mating and breaking apart the ice which makes up its homeland. The narwhal uses its tusk when faced by an obstruction, such as when ice covers most of the water surface, and the whale has no breathing hole.

The Narwhal and Bowhead both use their heads wisely in terms of how and where to break ice, and there is no denying the fact. The lessons learnt from them are on how we can find a solution even in the toughest of times, when our minds race in confusion, anger, sadness and panic, and to the whale, when there is a stray iceberg blocking its way or when they find no place for a breathing hole, and to pave new paths for oneself and others, breaking chucks of ice through the cold Arctic or breaking into new opportunities that we should use judiciously.

Think with our heads, pointed or blunt, strong or aerodynamic.

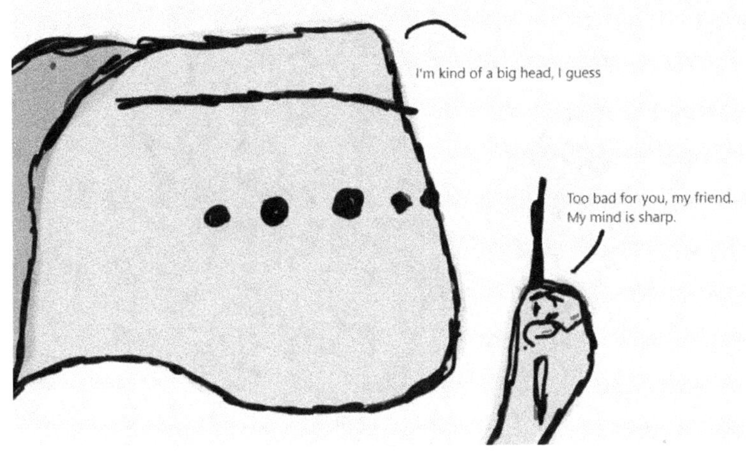
I'm kind of a big head, I guess
Too bad for you, my friend.
My mind is sharp.

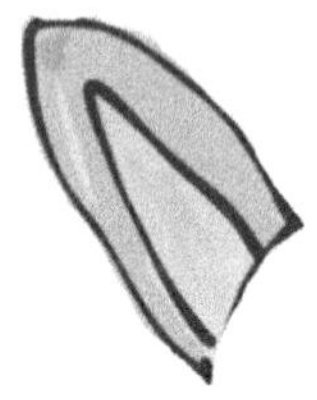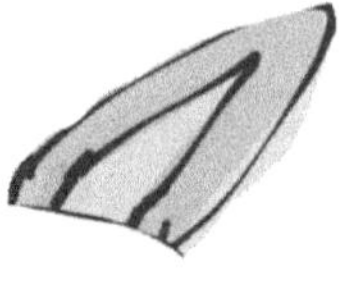

12. Fanatically Cunning Foxes

Bushy tail and crooked grin,

Deftly plotting crooked sin.

Tail all still and mouth open wide,

Look out, foxy will pounce onto your hide.

As sly as a fox. This refers to the fox and its nature of tricking everyone who dares to cross its path. The pointy ears, black and upturned snout and a long bushy tail. They are the signature features of a fox that sets them apart from the rest. It might be tricking a goat into jumping into a well, or devouring a runaway gingerbread man, the fox has long since been associated with crookedness, greediness, and cunningness. The fox is often depicted as the one who eats sheep, the one who finds the slyest way to deceive someone and other things that are deemed bad. Foxes are part of the dog family and live alongside humans in cities, towns and rural areas. Foxes are unpredictable in nature.

So, what are the lessons that we can learn from the fox? Though they may be sly, their smart minds have helped them live, and their uncanny nature has outsmarted even the smartest of prey, tricky to catch.

You know what? Tails suck! Just cut off yours, and you'll see what I mean. They just hang behind us, like long, snakelike gits trying to follow us............
You say that because you want the rest of us to be a tailless wimp like you!
How did he figure out?
That claim is rubbish!

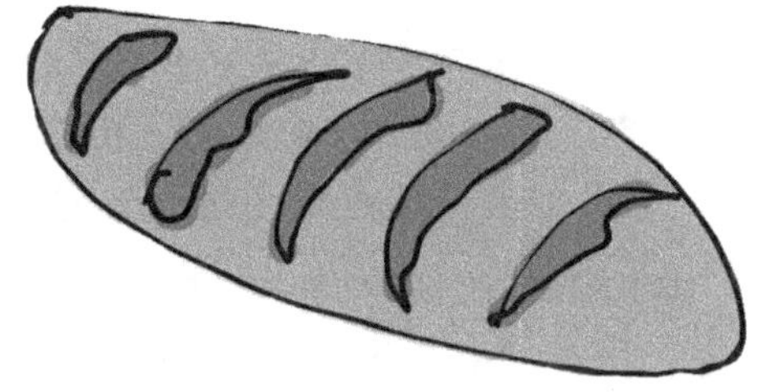

13. Yeast and Bread

At first, I'm paste without a taste,

*Then with a spoon, you roll me
out, rather in a haste,*

As you work on me, I get softer by time,

Until you set me into my mould,

And after baking, you get culinary gold.

Yeast is a single – celled fungus which needs warmth to rise. It helps dairy products ferment. And that's the main function of yeast. It also helps breweries ferment their beer, wine etc. It lets out carbon dioxide, which helps pastries become puffier. The basic ingredients of making bread are milk or curd, sugar, yeast and all-purpose flour. After we leave the dough for fermentation, which is when yeast kicks in. Yeast ferments the dough and when its size is just about right for you, put it in the oven, and set the temperature.

So, after you transfer your dough into its bowl, or mould, yeast helps the dough grow. Similarly, if we put our mind to something, the thing we would like to do is the mould, with its boundaries, and your willpower is like yeast, helping you grow bigger and better in the field. You may also be confined to some negative types of moulds, such as aggression, sadness or arrogance from whose borders you should break free. Likewise, never be confined to a single area. Grow your intelligence in different places, which can expand your views and can help you.

So mom, is this insignificant thing called yeast living? Can we keep it as a pet?
Huh! So you call me an INSIGNIFICANT pet, eh? After all the hard work I've been doing to make you pastries? No more breads for you, sonny!
YEAST

14. Ten o'clock on time

Time goes on like the rail below a train,

Through sunny plains and wicked rains,
Though many years may pass, and
things may fall into decay,

Time runs along, it will never fray

Punctuality is never bad. Being on time pays off later. Such punctuality is that of the ten o' flowers. They wake up at ten o' clock in the morning (Hence the name), a time when most people would agree that you should already be awake. The petals of the flower stretch themselves into the air in the morning, fresh from a long sleep. Late into midday, the petals start to lose interest staring at the sun. When the clock strikes four, the flower creeps back into their blanket of petals, shutting out light till ten next morning. So, why do these plants bloom only at63e a specific time? Well, these flowers have a biological clock (which is just a fancy word for having a sense of time) and because of this, they only bloom at specific timings, because they open up strategically at times when they feel they'll have an easier time pollinating. So what lesson can we learn from the ten o' clock?

Thinking strategically, planning carefully, and being punctual are things that the ten o' clock flower teaches us.

We
ten o' clocks
have a
biological
clock. It helps
us be on
time.

15. Ant's Antics

Small being, I am destined to be,

Big things, I'm told to do,

And though some of those tasks
might seem impossible for me,

If I don't do it, then in the world who?

And though you may not agree;

How many times have you seen
an ant carrying a crumb?

From your cake platter towards
their home, a grassy hump.

At the end of the day, tired from work,

And though it hurts, we are

not the one to whine,

And then over there, we pat
each other on the back,

For next morning we have to get up early,
and onto the next raid, we march in line.

"Small I may be, insignificant I am not" are the words that ants bear in mind. It is the motto that they live by, describing the power they wield despite their tiny size. The bite of a bullet ant is said to last an entire day. Despite the fact that they bite hard, ants are great team workers. They will go to any lengths, clambering up and scaling down walls with bits of food. They work hard to take their food to their homes. And even though ants are hard workers, there are also a couple of dummies among their species as well. Fire ants sleep up to 250 times every day, and most of these short naps last about one minute. They sleep at random points of the day. The ant civilisation is complex compared to other insects and can contest with our own. Their anthill colonies are huge apartment buildings that house millions of ants, each with a queen that rules over. A queen ant can live for over thirty years, which is a pretty long lifespan for an insect so small.

So what can we learn from ants?

Ants set their minds on things they want to do, and they work hard and reach their goal. Similarly, we mustn't slack off, but keep working hard. We can also learn to let go of other, less important things, rest, and ready ourselves for our next endeavour.

16. Cleaver Billed Crows

Their black wings fly in the wind,

Their determination, it doesn't unwind,

And though they're in unfamiliar grounds,

they're smart,

And though many miles, they travel,

Their home, they hold close to heart.

Each of us have our own experiences with crows. Those friendly neighbourhood watchmen look at us all day long from their perch high up in the sky, sometimes on electric poles or wires, sometimes on lamp posts. They look at us with merciless, black eyes, forever intimidating. They are related to ravens and jays, and both male and female of this species have little difference from each other. They are pretty smart, and allegedly, they can count up to five.

So, what can we learn from crows?

From crows, we can learn to think before making any move, independent living and fending for ourselves, to think out of the box and to make use of opportunities.

17. Grouper Cooperation

Over there, springs up a grouper fish,

And over, springs a moray eel,

Together they swim, together they fish,

Every ripple in the water they feel.

Deep in reefs and rocks, prey the
grouper has found,

And swoops in, the eel,

And it hunts down their prey like a hound,

And in the end, they share a

fish, brought to heel.

Collaboration. From the early days when cavemen worked together to bring down mammoths, to our days, when people work together to achieve something, it has been ingrained in our DNA forevermore. Well, animals too, use teamwork to get to their goals, and they sometimes do succeed. From lionesses in the Savannah who bring down zebras for food, to the simple gecko that we might find at our homes, who stick out their tongues, and capture small insects, to the grouper fish and moray eels, who we are talking about. Grouper fish and moray eels go hand in hand when it comes to hunting in groups. First, the grouper searches the area they are in and finds suitable prey. They then start making a grunting noise, and the moray eels, alerted by the grouper's grunting, appear on the scene and dive even into narrow openings to catch the prey.

As they have a very flexible body, they can navigate easily through the maze of tunnels and labyrinths. After they have tracked down and have successfully subdued the prey, they invite the groupers for dinner.

So, what can we learn from them?

Their weird, but reliable method, their ingenious cooperation, and their well-planned ways of catching their prey can teach us to be organized, to plan well before executing things, and to work well with others.

18. Sedentary Silkworm

Beautiful silk clothes, you sew and stitch,

Intricate patterns without a glitch,

But a man in the works, remaining unknown,

Is the silkworm, who should be
much better known

Chinese people were the first to practice the art of sericulture (Silk making). Over the years, it has spread to other places. The process of making silk starts with the silkworm, who feeds on mulberry leaves. After their vegan meal, they weave a cocoon of silk, in which they wrap themselves in. When this process is done, the people who are working on the silk boil the round/oval shaped cocoons to make it easier to pull out the threads of silk. After the silk is pulled out, it is first washed and then dyed, then woven into clothes. Before silk was discovered (a time when a silkworm was thought to be just another worm like any other) the silkworm would have a nap inside the cocoon and wake up as a moth. Today, the silkworms don't make it outside as moths. Now, silkworms are specifically bred for this purpose. As they live to make silk, they have lost all the abilities their species had wielded and are now dependent on us for food, as they are not free as they once were. From the silkworm, we can learn not to procrastinate, and not to waste our life away, but to use and live it to the best extent.

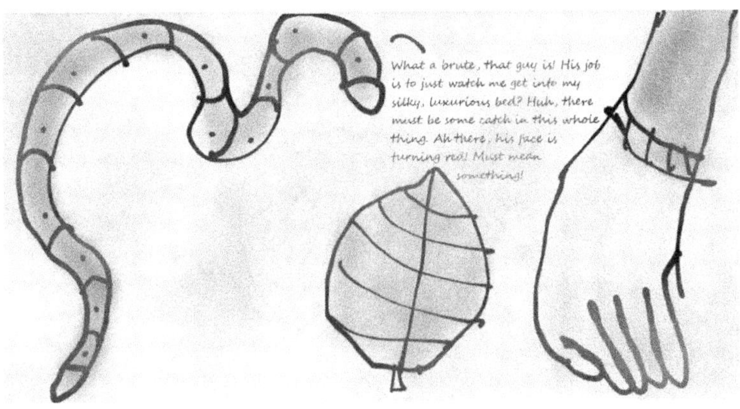
What a brute, that guy is! His job is to just watch me get into my silky, luxurious bed? Huh, there must be some catch in this whole thing. Ah there, his face is turning red! Must mean something!

19. The Ball Of Life

Dawn is my rise,

Dusk is my set.

Have you met another one,

Who could replace me best?

Sun

As you part your curtains, you see the Sun coming up into the sky, turning it purple. As you watch the Sun's ascend, you realize that a new day with new expectations has dawned. The Sun.

We associate power, light, brightness, greatness and all the possible positive thoughts with the Sun. We even set aside Gods and assign them the job of controlling the Sun. Eg: Ra, the Egyptian Sun God, Apollo, from Greek and Freyr from Norse mythology). The ancient tribes from many countries have offered prayers, sacrifices and much more to the Sun. The Sun teaches us punctuality, as it arrives on time, when it doesn't get held up by the clouds. And after a long day of work, you might go out for a walk and see the Sun, giving its final goodbyes to the moon and retiring for the night.

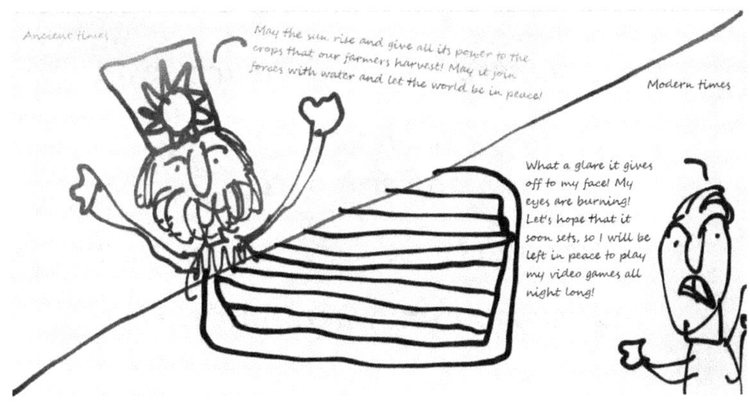

20. Resilient Lantana

Some plants are secluded much away,

*As they need much more and
can't afford to stay.*

But some plants need very little to survive,

And can grow anywhere, and thrive.

When an animal or plant takes over an area it didn't originate from, takes over the land and thrives, it is usually called an invasive species, and lantana is one of many such invasive species around the world. Lantana is not as appreciated in some countries as it is in others. The flowers of lantana grow in the shape of a bouquet, and are found in many shades of orange, red, yellow and white. Being native to South America, lantana was brought to India as an ornamental plant. If controlled, the plant can be safely grown, but in the absence of supervision, a few small bushes of Lantana can make a forest by itself. It is very fast growing, and due to its resilience and power to grow almost anywhere, controlling it, once it is a large bush is next to impossible. Lantana grows in huge, rather spiny bushes. Plant is a nuisance to farmers as the plant is poisonous to both humans and livestock. The power of lantana lies in its resilient nature, making itself able to grow in so many countries as an invasive species.

So, what can we learn from the lantana?

Wherever they go, the lantana plant makes their presence known; they grow big and wild, and take over, no matter what fences or walls stand in their way. So, we can learn to not be bound by restrictions, and to make our mark.

JOSHUA BEJOY

21. Robust Bougainvillea

Summer, rainy, autumn and winter,

All weather's harsh, plants are sure to wither,

Only the strongest will stay, only strongest

will stand,

The plants that stay, you meet heroes at hand.

Though plants are living things, they can't move or express their feelings. And as the question of survival arises, plants have rigged up a way to make food from Sun rays, and their roots dig deep down to find groundwater. While some plants need special care for their survival, there are several plants like the cactus, who store water in their bodies, and the eucalyptus, (which has long roots to suck water from afar). Likewise, the beautiful flowering plant bougainvillea also ensures its survival in its own way. It is resilient to hot and cold weather alike, and has long and powerful roots, which can make finding water look like a piece of cake. Its main feature is its strength to survive. The lesson we can learn from bougainvillea is its capacity to adapt in changing circumstances.

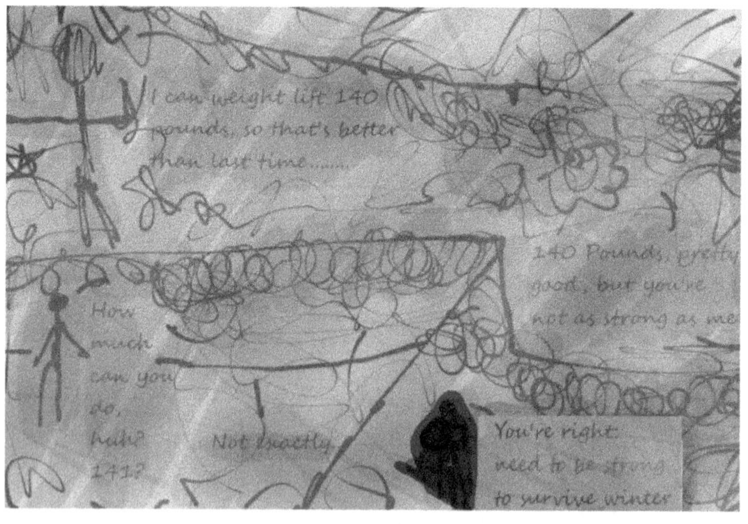

22. Smart Squirrels

Small I might be, you might not see,

Holes in trees I live to be.

Fruits and nuts I collect and keep,

Not waiting for the winter winds to sweep by.

So, whenever we go outside, we usually see these sights: The branches and leaves of trees swaying slightly, the sound of birds chirping, and the rustling sounds of squirrels swiftly zooming across the ground, and climbing up the trees. Squirrels may not strike as an animal with any importance at first sight, but the service that they render to nature is irreplaceable. As squirrels collect nuts for themselves, their families and other squirrels, they bury themselves to keep them safe from other squirrels. Naturally, they forget the many places that they buried their nuts. In due course, trees grow in the place where once the nut was carefully covered by a squirrel. There are about 250 different species of squirrels, and they are found all across the world, except for Australia and Antarctica.

So, at the end of the day, what can we learn from squirrels?

To be energetic, to have a friendly nature, to try to protect nature in whatever humble way we can and to practice sharing with others are qualities the squirrels teach us.

Mr. Nutcase, one last question: Can you show us the fruits of your labour that helped you secure your place as the world's richest squirrel?

DAILY REPORTER

Take notice, gentlemen! These nuts are the fruits of my labour! Hopefully, they'll last many winters to feed my family!

23. Snappers

Dare come close to me,

You better be gone by the time
I say one, two three,

And if you choose to stay,

Feel a bang, feel your head go lighter than hay.

Snapping shrimps are the two-inch gunslinger anomalies of nature who live underwater. Also known as the pistol shrimp, they live in coral reefs, where they make a burrow, and usually, live together with a useful roommate. So, for example, some snapping shrimp live with goby fishes. While the shrimp builds and takes care of the burrow, the goby fish acts as the security system, and warns the shrimp when danger is approaching. This kind of roommate-ship is called a symbiotic relationship. So, at the end of the day, what does the shrimp's snapper claw do? Well, the snapping claw, for which this shrimp is famously known, is nearly as big as the shrimp itself. The shrimp waits for little fishes to swim near it, and this is when things get fast. The shrimp opens a part of its snapper claw, lets some water in, puts the water under pressure and then shoots the water in one big blast; and the next thing, you know, is that the little fish is stunned and is shifted to the shrimp's dinner table.

At the end of the day, what are the lessons that we can learn from the snapping shrimp?

Well, the snapping shrimp teaches us to be friendly, to lend a hand, to share, to socialize, to have our own powers that sets us apart from others, and to plan strategically, so we get to our goals.

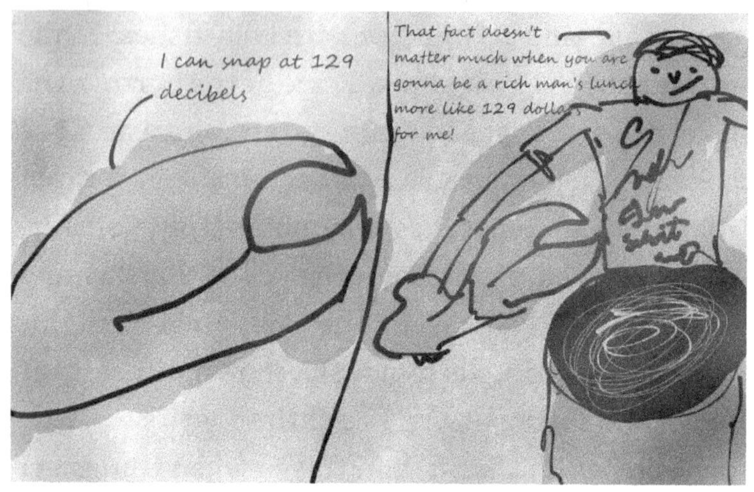

I can snap at 129 decibels
That fact doesn't matter much when you are gonna be a rich man's lunch more like 129 dollars for me!

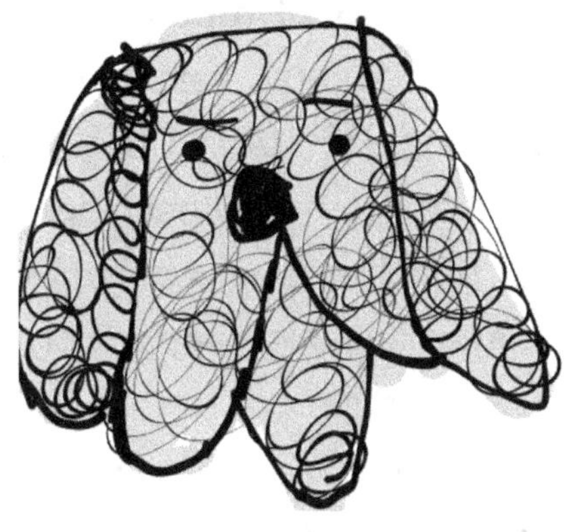

24. Canis Lupus Familiaris

Birds have beaks, fish have teeth,

Lions rip flesh, spiders suck food.

But then what does a dog do?

It has canines, of course!

Dogs are commonly known as man's best friend as they are one of the most loved pet animals (no offence meant to any other pet animal). The dog that we know today is descended from the wild wolves who lived in human company since the dawn of our civilisation. Humans began to practice agriculture about 10,000 years ago around the period when they also started the domestication of animals. Today's cow may have descended from the wild oxen that humans captured for food and used as farm animals. Dogs apparently had several traits that the first generation of farmers found highly useful, such as their fierce nature that was appreciated in hunting, and their unconditional love for their human friend. As time passed, humans studied and perfected the science of breeding and have created various new dog breeds. And now, different breeds of dogs are roaming the planet, each with its own diseases, temperament, psychology and use. Some are police sniffer dogs, while others are actors, hunters, therapy dogs and lap dogs. A handful of dogs have even gone all the way up to space.

The unconditional love that they provide us with, no matter what the situation, their loyal nature, and their friendly approach are lessons that we can learn from dogs.

You know what, great dane? You are not my brother, even if the humans think otherwise. I don't belive you are a dog at all! I'm a good old hound and I can easily prove that

So, my dear friend! I just can't belive the lie that you are a hound. What kind of a hound are you? A titch hound, probably!

?!!!

25. Web Weaver

My web is thin, my web is strong,

Made from a thing that you can't find about.

My web may be thin, but be warned,

Don't stick in your thumb, or you
will become insect dinner now.

From afar, spiders and their webs are nothing that might catch your eye. But as we move closer, we can see the delicate, thin and sticky strands that make up their web. The spider has two main kinds of silk: the sticky silk with which the spider builds its web and the silkier and softer silk it uses to wrap its prey tight and its own eggs, that is until the offspring come out. To catch dinner, the spider first makes a web using its sticky silk and then patiently waits for prey to cross paths with the spider, and land on the spiderweb and get stuck. When the prey gets firmly trapped inside the web, the insect starts struggling to get free, mostly by wriggling, and occasionally, ripping parts of the web in the process. Once the spider senses that there is a prey in the web, it approaches the struggling prey and injects a small dose of venom as a sedative and then, soon after, starts wrapping the prey in its soft silk. After the "packaging" is done, the spider proceeds to consume the prey. There are also some spiders who have no venom at all, while others have really potent venom, a few examples being the funnel web spider, black widow, banana spider (or Brazilian wandering spider) etc. The spider's goal is simple: Achieve by working hard and perseverance. As in the nursery rhyme, Itsy Bitsy Spider suggests, a spider will have to rebuild its web several times when rain, wind, hail or struggling insects rip away its web. The only way for the spider to not go to bed hungry is by building its web, waiting patiently for unsuspecting insects to get caught and then enjoy the fruits (or insects) of labour. The lesson that the spider teaches us is to never give up, but keep working until we reach our goals.

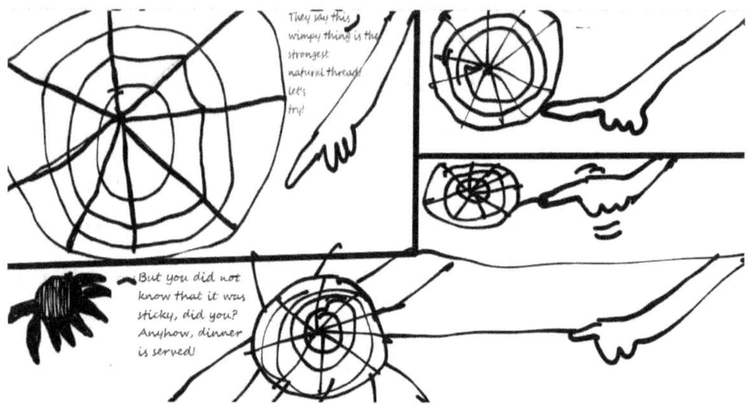

26. Sunshiny Sunflowers

Have you ever seen a flower,

So happy and so cheerful,

That it never seems to glower,

When seasons come and go,

It only seems to glimmer.

Sunflowers were first bred and cultivated by the Native American people for its seeds. Later, when European settlers came, they took sunflowers to Europe and cultivated them there. Now, sunflower seeds are available pretty much everywhere. Sunflowers symbolize wealth, happiness, positivity, brightness, loyalty etc. The flowering buds of young sunflower plants always tend to face the Sun and turn accordingly throughout the day as the Sun moves across the sky.

The lessons that we learn from the sunflower is to assimilate knowledge while we are young, by constantly engaging our minds with the sources of knowledge so as to enable us to lead a fruitful life. The other lesson we can learn from the sunflower is to be strong and shine as bright as the sun.

27. Troublesome Termites

From tall mounds of mud, they emerge,

And in different directions, they crawl,

In search of wood to purge,

To eat in parts, or to eat as whole.

Through grassy lawns, through
dry urban roads,

Through desert lands, and paths travelled least,

They find wood, and they destroy it in loads,

On mounds of wood, they feast.

"Dang, those termites are in town!" is the thought that passes through our mind when we see holes in our furniture. Although termites are a bother to many, they are actually good for the ecosystem (As long as the termite does not decide to make your home a makeshift ecosystem). It makes sure that the soil is fertile by burrowing, which lets air and water circulate through. Termites play a major role in decomposing dead trees, faeces and leaf litter. Its diet consists mainly of vegetative waste materials. With its ability to recycle dead wood and turn the soil fertile, it is one of nature's biggest rejuvenators. There is a queen for each colony of termites (which is a similarity that they share with ant colonies). Another similarity between the two is that termites also build huge mounds akin to anthills.

So, that can we learn from termites? As you know, termites are detested around the world, in spite of their valuable services to nature, because they feed on your furniture, clothing, books etc. The lesson to learn here is to do the thing that you feel is right to do, and not to let your point of view be biased by anyone else.

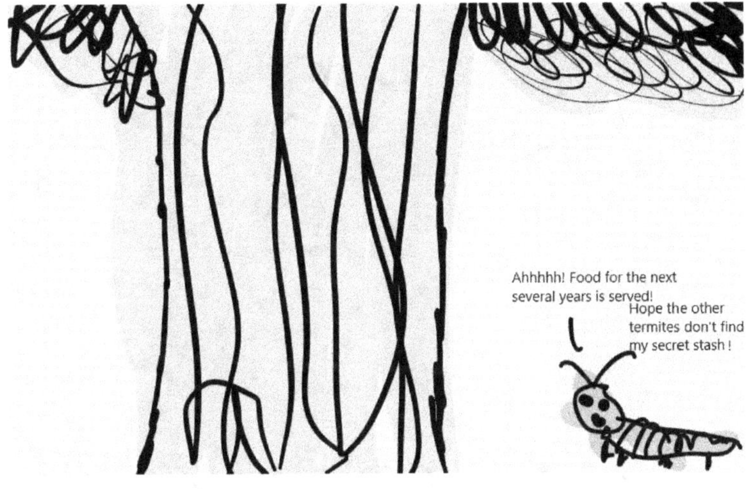
Ahhhhh! Food for the next
several years is served!
Hope the other
termites don't find
my secret stash !

28. The Breath of Life

Trees grow big and trees grow short,

Some grow crooked, while others grow straight,

*But one thing trees give you
can't find elsewhere,*

It is the oxygen, dead trees, you can't find.

Oxygen is an essential part of life. About 400 million years ago, trees started to appear on earth. Before that, the concept of trees was non-existent, and life forms lived in water, where there was a tiny amount of oxygen. Most of the life forms were microorganisms, which didn't require a lot of oxygen. So, when plants and trees got into the scene, they used Sun's light to synthesize food and let out oxygen as a by-product of that process. As the microorganisms began to evolve into more complex lifeforms, they started to move on to land, while some stayed put in water. The rest, as people put it, is history. Oxygen made its way around every nook and cranny, facilitating an atmosphere with more fresh air than anyone could ask for. Maintaining trees is now more important than ever before for our survival, as we are cutting down, polluting and making survival incredibly hard for trees. Even though trees take in carbon dioxide, we are giving out more CO2 than any number of trees can handle.

Trees teach us one thing: they provide us with oxygen, no matter what the place or situation. Just like that, we must be able to provide help to anyone, no matter where the place or situation is.

AHHHHH!
Nice produce this year, tree!
Thanks buddy! Its all fresh air all from the soul!

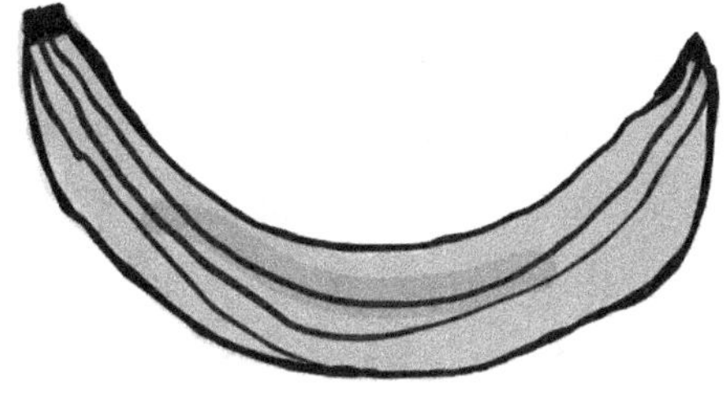

29. Chimps aren't Wimps...

The crack of a nut and the whip of a tail,

Falling leaves bring out the Sun's bright glare,

The bushels rustle and comes out a face,

*And then the monkey grins and
runs off for a race.*

Chimpanzees are our closest monkey relatives. It is thanks to them that we are now the species we are today. We evolved from the same family to become a more dominant species. However, we share about 90 percent of our DNA with them. Though chimpanzees are capable of walking upright, their broad hips give them a stooped appearance and they prefer to walk on all fours. The characteristics that helped our early ancestors survive and give birth to subsequent generations, were their hunter instincts, their proficient use of tools made of wood and stone (later moving on to many other sophisticated tools, the reason being the discovery of metal extraction, alloying and forging), their ability to learn from failures and their dominant behaviour, whereby everyone strives to be the best, which led to conflicts and wars to test each other's power.

And that is the best part. Our ancient ancestors learned from their mistakes and improved their technologies to make many great civilisations which rose and fell over the centuries, and each one of them played a pivotal role in shaping us the way we are living now.

You filthy ??!?!?!? animal you! Wait till I get you for stealing my sandwich
Didn't natural history teach you about extended family?

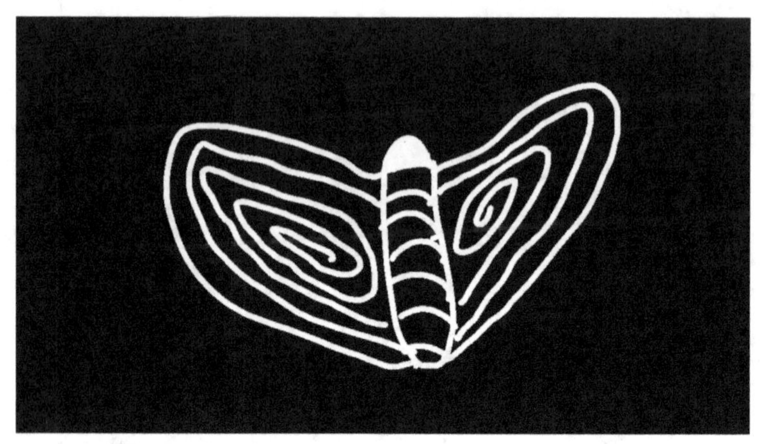

30. Butterflies as Butlers

The delicate breeze ruffles her wings,

As she collects honey from a
flower with purple rings,

Then she turns around, rather
startled at my sight,

And then she turned her back and
flew away with all her might.

Butterflies are insects from a family that includes moths. Their wings are colourfully decorated with shades of blue, light brown and red, and rarer colours such as deep purple and pale blue. Butterflies feed on nectar from flowers. They land on the flower's petals, uncurl their long, straw-like proboscis and sucks the nectar. In the process, a few pollen grains get stuck to the butterfly's legs. When it travels and sucks nectar from the next flower, a few of these pollen grains get deposited on it, facilitating pollination and thus giving birth to the next generation of plants.

The lesson that we can learn from butterflies is that we help others execute tasks which they are unable to do themselves (e.g., butterflies help pollinate, a job that flowers can't do themselves).

31. Camouflage Chamaeleon

Vibrant shades of red and blue,

Next time find me with a yellow hue,

Brown as bark and green as grass,

I'm a Chamaeleon, and when
it comes to colours,

I'm never at a loss.

Chameleons are strange creatures. They are one of those rare beings that can change the colour of their bodies. Though they cannot completely blend in with their surroundings, the chameleon can fairly disguise itself by manipulating the scales on its body. It is the strange way that these animals have found to survive. The average chamaeleon is about eight to sixteen inches long, with females being a little longer than males. A chamaeleon's diet consists of insects, which it catches using its long tongue. It creeps upon the prey and then releases its sticky tongue on the prey. A feature that helped chameleon to survive till now is its adaptability to avoid getting caught by other predators. The lessons that the chameleon teaches us are to be adaptive, to multitask (looking simultaneously in two directions counts), to have accuracy and such. In all, it is a creature to behold with its strangeness and eccentricity.

JOSHUA BEJOY

32. Mysterious Mimic Octopus

As rocks and reefs become scarce and few,

I move to the sea bed, which will
go away one day too,

But my crafty tricks and crafty thought,

Will keep me alive till I get caught.

Octopuses are no strangers to the world of mimicry. They can pretend to be rocks on the seafloor, squeeze into any tiny opening (as they don't have any bones) and can squirt ink to escape any approaching predators. These oddities and fantasies make the octopus special. Their species spans over three hundred different varieties, each with its own wonders. The largest species of octopus is the giant pacific octopus and the largest known specimen was around thirty feet long, while the smallest species wolfi octopus is only 2.5 centimetres in length. Among this eccentric array of sea creatures, the mimic octopus stands solitary, with its own skill setting it apart from the rest of its species. At first glance, it might seem like nothing much, only about two feet long, but you might mistake the octopus's black and white hide to be one of a sea snake. And that's where the mimic octopus has both an advantage and a disadvantage. It cannot squirt any ink which will obstruct the predator's view, but it can pretend to be one out of fifteen other creatures, which are usually poisonous. Anything from sea snakes to lionfish are on their list. When it is particularly hungry, it can pretend to be a mate for a crab and then devour the unlucky crab who got drawn to the octopus. Thus, the mimic octopus has become one of nature's most gifted tricksters (besides the fox).

The lesson we can learn from the mimic octopus is to take advantage of the circumstances, whether with a predator at your heels, or with a crab lunch to find.

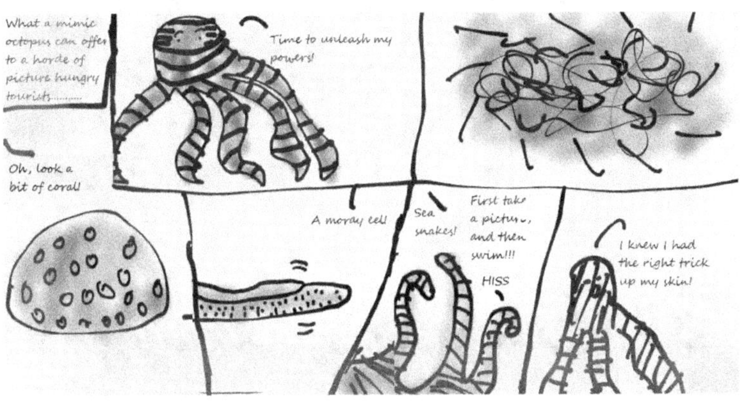

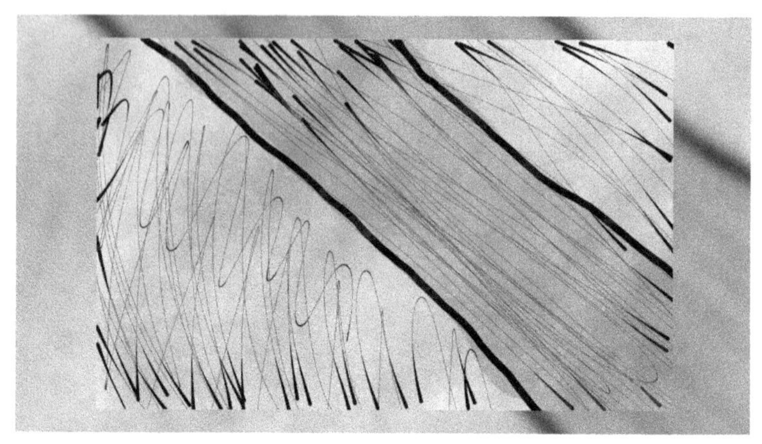

33. Everlasting Eucalyptus

Thin and tall, I stand alone,

My bark is grey from years of bore.

And though spring goes well and
summer comes harsh,

I worry not, as my big strong
roots will find a marsh.

Eucalyptus, when it comes to looks, might not be striking. It looks rather plain with its grey bark. You might think it's not even a tree. Eucalyptus trees aren't fast growing and are quite self-sufficient as their long roots travel searching for water. This in its turn, helps them survive harsh climates for long periods of time.

Eucalyptus, unlike how it might seem at first sight, is a very useful tree. Its leaves are very good air fresheners. Its oil is useful against respiratory illnesses, as an antiseptic against insect bites, small wounds and burns.

So, what can we learn from the eucalyptus?

Eucalyptus roots do long searches for water underground, and metaphorically, this tells us to work harder, until we reach the destination that we once thought was so far away.

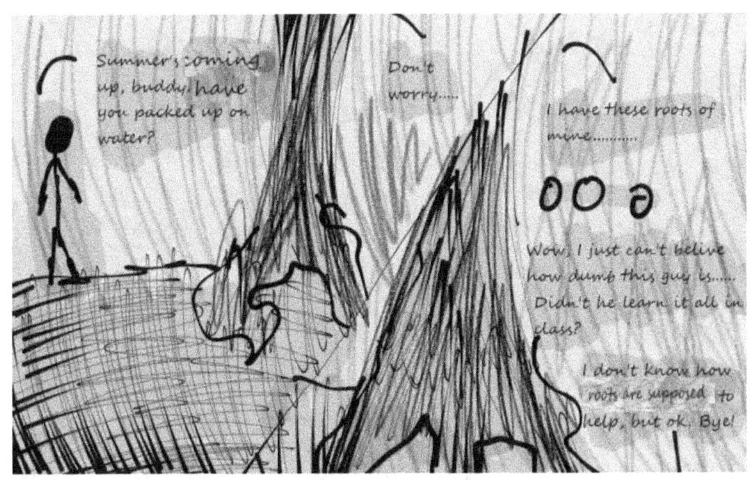

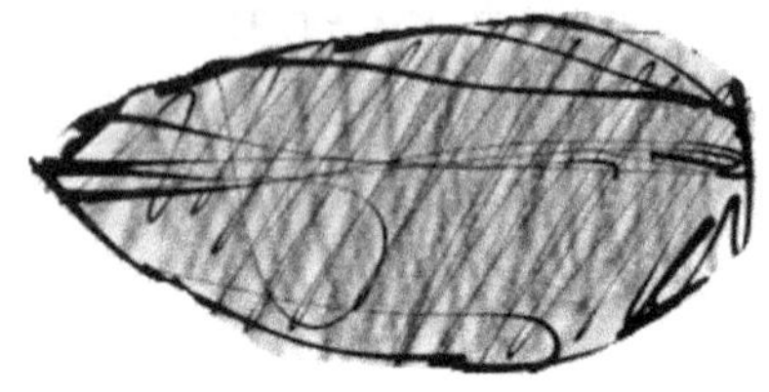

34. Simple Seeds

I grow atop a flower or plant,

I'm its child and ripe produce I shall grant,

With some soil and sunlight
and water in measure,

I shall bear fruit for you, with pleasure

A seed is an embryonic plant with a hard outer covering, and it is the main way of reproduction in plants, other than pollen, cutting a stem, and then setting it into soil etc. If provided with ample soil, sunlight, water and care, the seed will continue its journey into a full-grown plant. A seed starts to grow when a plant is old enough to produce offspring. In most plants, it happens so that the fruit or the flower is the reproductive part. The flower contains pollen grains, some of which fly away when wind blows, while some settle on flowers in the same plant.

So what can we learn from seeds?

A seed, such a small thing, grows into a plant, or a tree, hundreds, maybe thousands of times its size: it is a transition that is remarkable.

35. "Those Plants Need Some Pruning!"

Plants are pruned to keep in check,
That they are good and not in wreck.
Humans are pruned for their good in deeds,
So when they grow up, they are sure to lead.

Pruning is the process of cutting away a stem, leaf, branch or flower from a plant. Pruning is not to destroy the plant, but to make sure that it grows better. When a tree gets overly bushy with branches and leaves, the extra foliage blocks the sunlight essential for photosynthesis. The aim of pruning is to reduce the burden of the plant and make it a little freer. Pruning is done when a plant's leaf, branch or flower is dried, looks weak etc. It is done so that it does not spread to other parts of the plant.

Pruning should be done gently, not aggressively. Winter is preferable for pruning, as at that time plants are in hibernation and do not feel the loss of a few branches.

Pruning in humans means a person of good character. Pruning, like other such processes, has its disadvantages also. A plant is ever-changing. We can alter it in any way, cut it in any way or shape it in any way. However, after a certain age, people are independent personalities who are shaped into the person they are by their past. When we are young, mistakes can be easily corrected and it is easier to get rid of bad habits, as we have only started living our lives, while in a later age, a person develops a sense of personality and has to draw a decision oneself if it is needed or not needed to get rid of something in their personality. In short, be a good person. Change for the better of yourself and your future.

PLANT SCIENCE JOURNAL

STUDY- Pruning is another word for plastic surgery in plants.

Siccssor- a preffered tool for pruning

SENSATION! Pruning makes a plant grow better and lets it stay alive for a longer time.

They're wrong. Even trees need haircuts, don't they?

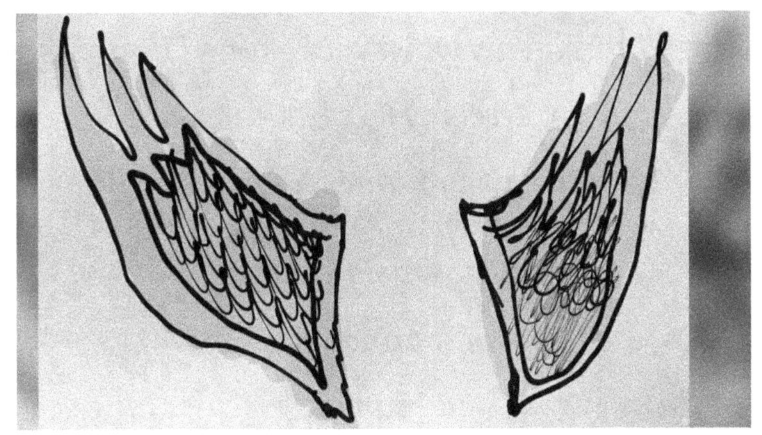

36. Falling Wings

Up from my nest, I peek out down,

I can see a car, I can see a town,

I can see a man, I can see a lady in a gown,

*My mother comes beside me
and tells me "Its time,*

*For you to go down to the lawn
and fly up high till dawn"*

I look down in terror of flight,

And slowly step front and deep a breath I take,

Until I spread my wings and I am wide awake,

I jump, I feel my legs leave my nest,

I feel the air around me, I felt myself
go down Flapping my wings hard,
lest I go crashing down,

I feel a gust of air and I flap my wings,

I fly up higher and I can see the door hinges,

I land on the lawn,

And I call out to mom,

"I've done it, now I can live alone!

Birds are one of the living creatures who have acquired flight skills. When they are born, all birds don't have feathers. They develop gradually, by about two weeks after the birds have hatched. Feathers are important for a bird's survival. Even though its main purpose is to help the bird fly, the function of plumage in flightless birds is to keep them warm, attracting others of its kind (in peacocks), camouflage and protection. In most flightless birds, the number of feathers has increased through evolution (The plumage of peacocks and ostriches have grown thick over the millennia and so has that of penguins' thick coat of feathers used for survival in the South Pole. There are two types of feathers in birds. The first type is contour feathers. This type of feather is found in the bird's tail, wings and back. It helps smooth out the body and provide an aerodynamic shape that is useful in flight. Under the contour feathers are the down feathers. They are softer and fluffier feathers, unlike the straight and broad contour feathers. They are the next layer after the bird's skin. Their main purpose is to keep the bird warm. After they hatch, birds are constantly hungry, and they slowly grow out of it at the end of their first few days of life. After the first week of their lives, they start opening their eyes, and flapping their wings, even though the feathers are still growing on them. After that, the parents of the birds go out for long periods of time. Each time, rather like policemen, they take their duties in shifts, like once when the mother bird sits for a few minutes to an hour, while the father bird is out looking for food and vice versa. While both of the birds have to respect each other's wishes and must synchronize with the other, I have a feeling that both of them have a long eye for the more peaceful seat above their offspring. When the chicks are about a couple weeks to a month or two old, they (depending on how many offspring the couple has given birth to) will surely capsize the nest as they are fully grown adults now. They no longer need food nor support from their parents. This is when the time comes for the parents to persuade their child to leave the house.

Making the small bird go away from home too early is not the best thing, as it can get injured and could die. But letting the child stay and only go after a longer period of time, the bird can become lazy and can become dependent on others, and might get too used to the homely comforts of unlimited food and comfort.

This is where the bird's parenting skills come into play. They make sure that their offspring is mature enough to sustain the weight of the outside world. In the first week of living outside, the parents will monitor the child from a distance. After a few days, the parents leave the scene forever, and they will probably never meet again.

So, what can we learn from the bird and its offspring?

Even though they are normal animals who we encounter every day, there is a lot that we can learn from them. Birds try to make good birds out of their offspring. They want to see their children grow up into birds who can live to be self – sufficient and independent. And that is the biggest lesson we can learn from them.

Acknowledgements

I would like to thank Dr. G. Ravikanth, scientist at ATREE Bengaluru, who kindly provided the picture for the book cover. My mother, Suma Sunny, gave me the inspiration to write this book. I thank my brother Jerome, my father, my grandparents, and my aunt, for their love and support.